LIFE ON THE INTERNATIONAL SPACE STATION

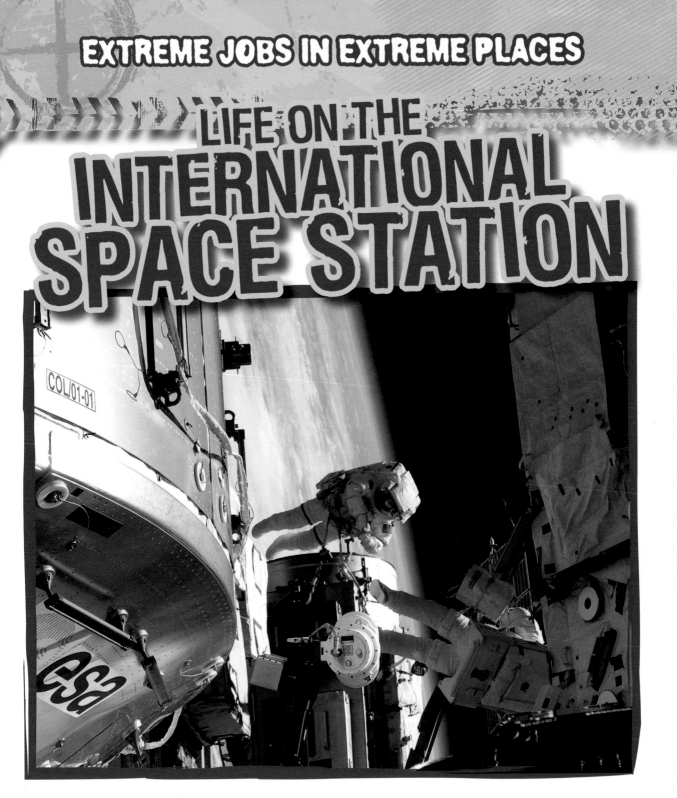

By Maria Nelson

Gareth Stevens
Publishing

Please visit our website, www.garethstevens.com. For a free color catalog of all our high-quality books, call toll free 1-800-542-2595 or fax 1-877-542-2596.

Library of Congress Cataloging-in-Publication Data

Nelson, Maria.
 Life on the International Space Station / Maria Nelson.
     p. cm. — (Extreme jobs in extreme places)
 Includes index.
 ISBN 978-1-4339-8508-9 (pbk.)
 ISBN 978-1-4339-8509-6 (6-pack)
 ISBN 978-1-4339-8507-2 (library binding)
 1. International Space Station. 2. Astronautics—International cooperation—Popular works. 3. Manned space flight—Popular works. I. Title.
 TL797.N45 2013
  9.44'22—dc36

                          2012031425

First Edition

Published in 2013 by
Gareth Stevens Publishing
111 East 14th Street, Suite 349
New York, NY 10003

Copyright © 2013 Gareth Stevens Publishing

Designer: Andrea Davison-Bartolotta
Editor: Therese M. Shea

Photo credits: Cover, pp. 1, 4, 10, 20, 21, 22, 23 NASA via Getty Images; pp. 5, 12, 24 Stocktrek Images/ Getty Images; pp. 6, 7, 8, 9, 11 (inset), 13, 16, 17, 19, 25, 27 courtesy of NASA via Wikimedia Commons; p. 11 NASA/Science Source/Getty Images; p. 14 PremiumVector/Shutterstock.com; p. 15 Encyclopedia Britannica/UIG/Getty Images; p. 27 (inset) Maxim Marmur/AFP/Getty Images; p. 28 iStockphoto/Thinkstock; p. 29 Roberto Gonzalez/Getty Images.

Interactive eBook credits: pp. 4-5, 20-21, 22-23 NASA via Getty Images; pp. 6-7 Onyx Media, LLC/Getty Images Editorial Footage/Getty Images; pp. 8-9 Bruce Weaver/AFP/Getty Images; pp. 10-11 footage courtesy of NASA.org; pp. 12-13 NASA/Photo Researchers/Getty Images; pp. 14-15, 16-17, 18-19, 24-25 courtesy of NASA via Wikimedia Commons; pp. 26-27 stock footage provided by MovingImages/ Pond5.com; pp. 28-29 Stocktrek Images/Getty Images.

Printed in the United States of America

CPSIA compliance information: Batch #CW13GS: For further information contact Gareth Stevens, New York, New York at 1-800-542-2595.

CONTENTS

Words in the glossary appear in **bold** type the first time they are used in the text.

ALL ABOARD!

Right now, six people are living and working aboard a huge structure that **orbits** Earth more than 15 times a day. They're crewmembers on the International Space Station (ISS). If you look up at the right time, you might be able to see their home!

The brave men and women who have set foot on the ISS come from all over the world. Crewmembers have included astronauts trained by NASA (National Aeronautics and Space Administration) and the ESA (European Space Agency) as well as Russian **cosmonauts**. What's it like living in space? It can be pretty extreme!

2011 ISS crew and visiting NASA astronauts

A BRIEF HISTORY

Construction of the International Space Station began on November 20, 1998. The United States and 15 other countries have been part of its building and operations. The first crew to live there arrived in 2000. In 2009, the ISS became fully operational with its first six-person crew.

WHO'S UP THERE?

Have you ever wanted to be an astronaut? Hundreds of people apply to NASA's training program. Only a few are selected about every 2 years. Those who are chosen come from a variety of backgrounds. Some have worked in medicine or scientific **research**. Others are members of the military.

Everyone who trains to live and work aboard the ISS has to have some knowledge of all the tasks that need to be done. But previous experiences—like working as a computer scientist or **engineer**—make an astronaut especially good at one or two jobs on the station.

HOUSTON, WE HAVE TRAINEES

The extreme work of ISS NASA crewmembers begins with 1 to 2 years of astronaut training in Houston, Texas. This includes classes about the computer systems on the ISS as well as physical challenges such as **scuba** training. Eventually, astronaut candidates learn how launch, flight, and orbit feel in the Shuttle Mission **Simulator**.

From preparing food to dealing with accidents, astronauts are trained in every kind of situation they might encounter aboard the ISS.

More than 200 people have visited or lived on the ISS. In 2011 and 2012, six astronauts flew up to the ISS to become its new crew.

Before becoming astronauts, these crewmembers worked in fields that prepared them well for the tough work on the ISS. Cosmonauts Oleg Kononenko and Sergei Revin worked as engineers. Astronaut Don Pettit worked in a lab studying **gravity** and performing space-related experiments. Gennady Padalka served in the Russian Air Force, and Joseph Acaba is a geologist and a former US Marine. André Kuipers, an ESA astronaut, is a doctor who served in the Royal Netherlands Air Force.

front row from left: Don Pettit, Oleg Kononenko, André Kuipers
back row from left: Joseph Acaba, Gennady Padalka, Sergei Revin

MIR

The ISS isn't the first space station in which people have lived and worked. In 1986, the Mir space station was sent into orbit. Its first inhabitants were Russian cosmonauts. More than 100 people from different countries lived on Mir until it was brought back to Earth in 2001.

WHICH WAY IS UP?

The weightless feeling you get when floating in water is close to what astronauts feel aboard the ISS. It's caused by very low gravity, or microgravity. Forces don't pull on people or objects as on Earth, so there's no "up" or "down" on the ISS. Heavy objects are easy to move. This can take some getting used to!

ISS crewmembers often feel sick to their stomach or get headaches when they first encounter microgravity on the ISS. It also changes how blood moves around the body. Crewmembers' faces look puffy and their legs look skinnier as more blood gets moved to the upper body.

At first, ISS crewmembers bump into walls as they get used to moving in microgravity. Sometimes they use straps or handles to keep themselves in place.

RUNNING IN SPACE

Exercise is an important part of living on the ISS. Each day, the crew runs on treadmills or rides bikes using special straps to hold them in place. Though it looks silly, these workouts keep the astronauts from losing too much bone or muscle while on their mission.

NIGHT OR DAY?

Have you ever been woken by the sun shining through your window? Imagine that happening every 90 minutes! As the ISS orbits Earth, the sun rises and sets about 16 times in 24 hours. It's hard to know when it's night or day. To help them get enough rest, crewmembers are each scheduled for 8 hours of sleep a day.

The ISS has two small cabins about the size of closets for crewmembers to sleep in. Crew also have sleeping bags that attach to the wall. But some crewmembers use microgravity to float around the station while sleeping instead!

STAYING IN ORBIT

Astronauts live aboard the ISS for weeks or months at a time. Members of space shuttle teams who are just there for repairs or to drop off supplies only spend about 2 weeks on the ISS. ISS crewmembers are often stationed in orbit for as long as 6 months.

Some crewmembers wear earplugs to block out the sounds of fans, computers, and other people when they sleep.

STICKING TO THE PLAN...OR TRAY

When you're hungry, you can just grab a snack. For those living on the ISS, even that takes work! First, each astronaut has a meal plan to follow. This helps them take in the right **nutrients**. Second, microgravity doesn't allow someone to just open a bag of popcorn. Instead, each food item is packaged by itself. The crew prepares and eats one item at a time or attaches the packages to a tray so they stay put.

Meals are important for another reason. They're scheduled time for the crew to hang out. Each astronaut is part of the ISS community and needs to feel at home.

PLANNING THE MENU

When preparing for months on the ISS, astronauts help choose what foods they'll eat. They even get to taste it ahead of time! Right now, most of the astronauts are American or Russian, so half the food is American—like macaroni and cheese—and half is Russian—like beet soup.

astronaut food

Microgravity makes astronauts' senses of taste and smell weaker. They use a lot of hot sauce on their food!

15

KEEPING CLEAN

It may sound funny, but the ISS has bathrooms, too. What happens to the waste? When astronauts flush the toilet, a **vacuum** system sucks solid waste into a storage system that's emptied later.

Urine, or liquid waste, may be sent into space to burn up in Earth's atmosphere. Some is recycled into water for the crew to use! While that might seem gross, it's an important process because the crew can only bring so much water to the ISS at a time. The crew also saves water by using wipes to clean themselves.

the Zvezda section, where waste facilities are located

HEALTHY TEETH

Just like you have to brush your teeth every day, astronauts have to keep their teeth clean. They can't run a toothbrush and toothpaste under water at the bathroom sink. So their toothpaste is made especially to help save water on the ISS.

This is what the toilet system on board the ISS looks like.

THEY'VE GOT A JOB TO DO!

The ISS's main purpose is research. Altogether, the crewmembers log about 160 hours a week doing experiments. From studying the effects of medicines to tracking pollution swirling around Earth, crewmembers work with scientists on the ground to learn more about space, our planet, and the human body.

Did you know the crew of the ISS is the subject of an experiment, too? Their bodies are closely watched to find out how they act in microgravity. Even their waste is studied to see what nutrients they need more or less of while working in space. This knowledge can help future astronauts live "off planet."

HELPING HUMANS

Some of the studies done on astronauts on the ISS help us here on Earth. Scientists learn about aging as well as bone and muscle loss, which can help older people. Experiments about harmful **bacteria**, such as salmonella, have shown that they grow well in space. This knowledge might help us, too.

ISS crewmembers have certain hours they must work. But sometimes they have to check on experiments during their off hours so the work is done right.

It took more than 40 flights and 13 years to bring all the pieces of the ISS into space. The first crews that lived on the ISS had a big job: putting the pieces together! Now that the ISS is fully assembled, the crew takes care of the station. They update computer systems and make sure **equipment** is in good working order. They even have to clean!

While this isn't always the most exciting work, the astronauts know it's important since, for a few months at least, the ISS is their home. Besides, part of maintaining the ISS is pretty exciting—the spacewalk!

OUTSIDE THE ISS

ISS crew, like space shuttle astronauts, train for spacewalks, or extravehicular activities (EVAs). Perhaps the most extreme job on the space station, an EVA takes a crewmember out into space. Sometimes, they need to repair or install a part on the ISS. They might also work with the giant robot arm attached to the ISS!

Mission Control keeps a
careful watch on the ISS.
They let the crew know
what maintenance needs
to be done.

WHAT TO WEAR

Most of the time, ISS crewmembers are in the controlled conditions of the space station. They wear comfortable clothes that they change every 3 days. Then, they throw them away!

An ISS crewmember's most extreme situation calls for a pretty extreme wardrobe. Spacewalks require an astronaut to wear a spacesuit. The suit supplies oxygen for the astronaut to breathe and keeps the body at the right pressure. Each spacesuit can be changed to fit an astronaut's needs. They're worn for about 25 spacewalks before they're returned to Earth to be cleaned and repaired.

The latest spacesuits have fingertip heaters, helmets with lights, and radios so the astronauts can talk to each other from outside the ISS.

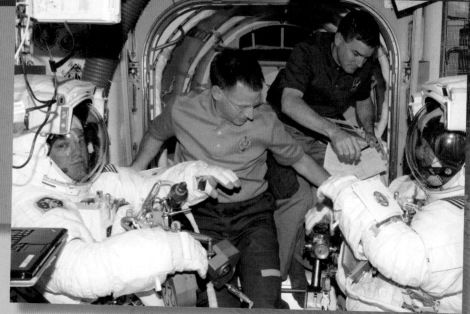

REMEMBERING EARTH

Crewmembers aboard the ISS can't have many personal items with them. However, they bring pictures and other small items. Most pictures are of their families and friends. Others include scenes that remind them of life on Earth, such as mountains or big open fields.

23

DOWNTIME

ISS crewmembers spend their free time doing many of the same things you do. They exercise, play cards, and watch movies together. There's not a lot of privacy on the ISS. Hobbies such as reading or listening to music with headphones can give hardworking crewmembers needed alone time, too. Some crewmembers do their own experiments or take pictures of space. One crew even took an electric piano with them!

Astronauts get homesick sometimes. Crewmembers spend a lot of time keeping in touch with their families and friends at home. They e-mail and even talk to them.

BORING OR BEAUTIFUL?

Many astronauts report that they spent some of their free time looking out the window! While that might not sound like much fun to you, astronauts can watch Earth spinning through space. It's hard to get sick of that view!

A Russian cosmonaut sends news to his family back on Earth.

SAFETY FIRST

Working aboard the ISS can be extremely dangerous. However, astronauts are prepared for most risky situations. If an astronaut becomes unattached from the station during a spacewalk, the spacesuit has a jetpack to help them fly back. Astronauts carry extra oxygen just in case there's a tear in a spacesuit, too.

In 2003, seven astronauts died when the space shuttle *Columbia* broke into pieces as it entered Earth's atmosphere. This reminded NASA of the many problems that could occur on missions and on the ISS. For about 2 years, ISS construction stopped as extra safety measures were put in place across all NASA's space programs.

A QUICK EXIT

Astronauts training to live and work on the ISS know it can be dangerous. But how many jobs do you know that have a "lifeboat"? Russian Soyuz spacecrafts bring the crew to the ISS. At least one remains docked there in case the astronauts need to leave the ISS quickly.

In 2010, a crewmember named Garrett Reisman was stuck outside the ISS on the robotic arm for 25 minutes when a computer caused the arm to stop working.

Soyuz spacecraft

WORKING TOGETHER

Crewmembers aboard the ISS have one of the coolest jobs in the universe! It's also one that can be lonely and scary. For months at a time, the crewmembers see only each other. While this creates a tight-knit community, it's hard to have such limited privacy. Astronauts miss their families, homes, and wide-open spaces, too.

However, the ISS crew is a well-trained group of astronauts who help each other through tough days of staring into the blackness of space. They recognize their work is important. Who knows? What we learn from the ISS crew today could help us live "off planet" tomorrow!

A FUTURE IN SPACE?

Though the ISS has only been completed for a few years, its end has already been discussed. The ISS will continue working until at least 2020. As astronauts learn and create new space machinery every year, the ISS could become outdated. What will the next space station be like?

The SpaceX Dragon lifts off in May 2012. SpaceX was the first private company to send a spacecraft to the ISS.

GLOSSARY

bacteria: tiny creatures that can only be seen with a microscope

cosmonaut: a Russian astronaut

engineer: someone who plans and builds machines

equipment: tools, clothing, and other items needed for a job

gravity: the force that pulls objects toward the center of a planet or star

nutrient: something a living thing needs to grow and stay alive

orbit: to travel in a circle or oval around something, or the path used to make that trip

research: studying to find something new

scuba: a tool used for breathing underwater, consisting of a container of air and a mouthpiece

simulator: a piece of equipment built to copy the features of something

vacuum: something that creates a sucking force

FOR MORE INFORMATION

Books

Holden, Henry M. *The Coolest Job in the Universe: Working Aboard the International Space Station.* Berkeley Heights, NJ: Enslow Publishers, 2013.

Tagliaferro, Linda. *Who Walks in Space? Working in Space.* Chicago, IL: Raintree, 2011.

Whittaker, Helen. *Living and Working in Space.* Mankato, MN: Smart Apple Media, 2011.

Websites

The International Space Station
www.esa.int/esaKIDSen/SEMZXJWJD1E_LifeinSpace_0.html
Read more about the International Space Station, astronauts, and some fun space facts.

NASA Kids' Club
www.nasa.gov/audience/forstudents/k-4/index.html
Play games and read stories about astronauts and space.

Space Station Orbital Tracker
spaceflight.nasa.gov/realdata/tracking/index.html
Find out where the space station is right now using this cool tracker.

INDEX